Mary, Dear Mary

(What's Growing in Your Garden?)

Gail Ruth Peterson

ISBN 978-1-68526-959-3 (Paperback)
ISBN 978-1-68526-960-9 (Digital)

Covenant Books
11661 Hwy 707
Murrells Inlet, SC 29576
www.covenantbooks.com

I thoroughly enjoyed reading *Mary, Dear Mary* and highly recommend it to anyone who needs inspiration and help to navigate through seasons of life such as grief and uncertainty, with hope and the pursuit of dreams. The poem is beautiful and a wonderful reminder of God's amazing love for each of us. One of my favorite parts of the book is about how the poem *Mary, Dear Mary* came to be, and how she wept when she read it back to herself for the first time, realizing she was about to embark on a new journey with God's guidance.

While Gail's story is heartbreaking at times, her message is positive, full of hope, and provides a great opportunity for us to learn from her journey. In addition, her story serves as a reminder for us to open our hearts to God by asking for guidance and being thankful for the blessings in our lives, even those we may not understand or comprehend.

There are questions in the book that we are encouraged to answer to help us develop our future paths, considering our unique skills and gifts. These questions, along with biblical references (at the end of the book), provide a foundational stepping stone to begin our next journey. I am thankful for Gail's inspiration and guidance in her book and look forward to learning and growing as I answer the questions and dig deeper into my purpose on earth in the next season of my own life.

Marci McClure
Director, Benefits
Womble Bond Dickinson (US) LLP

This book couldn't have come at a better time because I am approaching a major crossroads in my life and desperately need divine guidance. Like the author, I have been in a lucrative career; however, it leaves me feeling like I'm burying my God-given gifts, talents, and purposes in trade for money.

Gail's creativity, life, and writing will inspire you as they have me since the day I met her. This book is one that you'll want to read again and again, each time more slowly, to spend time reflecting on the poem, answering Gail's questions, and pondering my identity in Jesus as she describes at the end of the book.

You want to keep tissues nearby and pray for an open heart so God may lead you to His purposes for your life. Many thanks, Gail, for your obedience in stepping out of the boat and onto the water.

Kelley Gallagher, RN

Mary, Dear Mary is a delight to read and ponder. It assures us that it is possible to develop a meaningful, purposeful, joy-filled path in life after major upheavals. Not only does Gail let us know we can

iv

work through grief and chaos in our lives, but she also suggests ways we can explore our options before deciding which path to take. The trials and course of her own experiences and faith journey, her encouraging words, and the Scriptures all work together like a workbook that allows us to sort through the steps and preparation we need to move in a new direction.

Diane Voliva
Artist, Skin Care Advisor

This book is incredible! It gives people hope and the motivation to never give up on their dreams—no matter how big or small. She also points out that because it's so easy to lose sight of our dreams, we can become unaware of the seeds we're planting or could be planting until someone reminds us of a vision or passion we once wanted to pursue.

Gail insists we be persistent, never to give up seeking the Lord for all things. I love the Scriptures she gives us to reflect upon after the poem, for they remind all of us of who we truly are in Christ.

Marlene Straley
Client Care Coordinator
Meals on Wheels of Horry County Inc.

To Jenn Depo

I owe so much to you, dear friend. You believed in me before anyone else. You made yourself available for phone calls, texts, and messages at any hour of the day or night.

It is amazing how we became friends in the first place—truly a God-story in itself! And though we met in a different town than where we resided, we soon discovered we lived around the corner from one another! I love how we both recognize now all the ways and reasons God put our lives together.

You not only gathered a village around me in those early days after Mike passed away, but you introduced me to my new UK friend, Ray, who introduced me to Rebecca, who became my business coach. Who knew (besides God) that it would take an international team of people to work with me? Thank you for being like a twin sister. It will always blow my mind that we so often think the same things at the same time. Are you sure we didn't develop in the same womb?

To Lee Ellen

You are all ears and an encouraging sounding board. You're an angel with a smile so big it glows through the receiver of my cell phone! Thank you for asking me what I'm up to each week and for full-blown enthusiasm and excitement over every single task I describe. You told me once you are a born encourager and—my, oh my—what an encourager you are, and so much more. No matter where our paths take us in the days ahead, I hope our ways continue to cross for however many days and years the Lord sees fit to give us on earth. I'm blessed to call you friend.

To Rebecca Adams

The first two words that I think of when I think of you are *amazing* and *eeeeek!* because you say these every time I share a new vision, plan, or proposal. You have been a huge encouragement to me, and you're so resourceful! Not only were you my coach in business, but you also became a sweet friend as we share in our losses this year—my husband and your mum. I love that we have also been an encouragement to one another in our grief journeys.

You only told me what to do twice, and both times, you were so wise. You only offer assistance in explaining how and when I could best fulfill all the ideas I present to you. I so appreciate your experience and resourcefulness!

The two things you ever told me to do is to be kind to myself (I need that reminder) and to seek God's divine downloads. I love that description because there have been so many times this year that my direction in life has truly felt revealed by divine downloads.

Thankfully, you have the mechanical experience I needed to move forward. I wouldn't be where I am now without you. I'm thankful that God knew what I needed when I suggested to Mike two years ago that I needed a business coach! I believe God was preparing me then for the day I'd meet you!

To Ana

It means more to me than you'll ever know that you would give your blessing to my gradually leaving your team of health coaches to pursue what is for me, a bigger dream. For you, we both knew that at least for a while, that meant we would both lose income and spend less time talking with one another each week. Perhaps some weeks, you might wonder, scratch your head, or question if I know what I am doing. But don't worry, I've done the same thing this year—again and again, yet here I am, fulfilling the dream!

To Mom

I know you felt like I should take the safer road and not let go of a profitable business that could easily support our new home and life together. I understand your mother's heart but appreciate you trusting me as I described my plans and dreams. You help me as best you can and pray that I follow what I believe is God's lead in all this.

I love that you always stop what you're doing to listen to me read something I've written. I love getting to know you again in our later years of life. It seems we're more like girlfriends these days because we laugh so much, but still, you always have your mother's heart. Who knew how much I needed that more than ever this year!

To my sister, Nance

Thank you for your monthly visits. Each week you're here, you gladly help Mom, help around the house, and give me time away to write or paint. I'm not sure you fully grasp or understand what I plan to do, but your faith in me is remarkable. How can I ever repay you all the time and energy, even the fears you've faced in your own life, to provide me with the time to work and also to rest from the many responsibilities I no longer get to share with my hubby.

To Kerry and Marlene

Thank you for giving me "white space" to breathe, think, reflect, and ask the question, "How did I get here?" It's funny that I had to explain that I knew how I got to your home, but I couldn't figure out how my life became so chaotic in the few months after Mike died.

Thank you for helping me sort out my thoughts and think about my dreams and what was best for my health, family, and life in the future without Mike. Thank you also for your continued support in my work and ministry. It's amazing how much our relationship has grown this year. I'm forever grateful for you both.

It still blows my mind when I receive a message, comment, text, or phone call from one of you thanking me for a morning Facebook post. It's hard to believe that reading them is your second task after grabbing your cup of coffee each morning!

So, friends, you should know that your encouragement fuels my passion for writing, dreaming, and working toward what I believe God desires for my life. It is the reason I pray daily for God to use me. I hope that in the remaining years of my life, God will provide many opportunities for me to offer hope and build faith in the lives of those called to fulfill their part in His kingdom. And I pray more and more of you will join me in this quest, this calling in these desperate times.

Contents

Introduction.. xv

Part One
Prelude...1

Part Two
Mary, Dear Mary...................................15

Part Three
Time to Reflect 26

Introduction

Mary, Dear Mary is a poem. It has many layers of life lessons and spiritual significance. But the story behind it is just as meaningful.

I wrote the poem a few months after the death of my second husband. I was trying to figure out what my life was supposed to look like after his death and finally had a plan. But as relieved as I was to have a plan in place, I realized the story might give just as much hope to anyone reading, especially those currently amid chaos and confusion.

It's become pretty normal, though, for me to live my life out loud. I do this for a reason—well, maybe a few. But the first reason is that I do not consider my life my own.

You see, I was once a little girl with a dream to meet my real daddy one day. Then, in 1994, on a particular Sunday in November, I realized my Heavenly Father fulfilled everything I imagined my biological father would be—and more! So I surrendered my life to Jesus, sensing that I had immediately changed that day and that God had a plan for my life. Now anything that happens in my life is a result of Christ in me. My life is His story; He is my testimony.

My dad and me 2013.

(Side note: I did meet my father, Fred, in 2013. A sweet relationship continues to grow between us!)

Second, I want to be an inspiration, a beam of hope and light, a witness of what Jesus can do in the life, heart, and mind of anyone willing to let Him in. It is not hard or complex. Jesus offers the gift of life, and He gives us unlimited access to our Heavenly Father in a most intimate relationship. A genuine relationship with Him is not always comfortable or easy, but watching how He orchestrates our lives is remarkably ingenious!

Finally, I want to point out that the seeds I describe in the poem, *Mary, Dear Mary*, are not just goals and plans. Oftentimes, seeds are dreams that sit in a dark place for a long time. In many cases, it seems the soil may get turned over many times before the dream sprouts. In my case, it's taken years for many situations and circumstances to come together to prepare the perfect condition for growth. May that be ingrained in your mind so you won't give up on your pursuit!

When you ponder the various seeds described in the poem, carefully consider the seeds you sowed in the past that did not produce a good harvest. You can't keep planting the same things and expect different results. Until the past year or two, I didn't believe I would ever be very good at anything. I look back now and see I unknowingly planted seeds of doubt in every endeavor.

What do you think were the results? You're correct if you guessed it was not an abundant harvest! I now see the need to plant seeds of confidence in God's love, that He will provide everything I need along the way, and it is not only okay to accept every gift, but darn right necessary if I want my life to honor Him!

God loves you, and if He has a plan for your life, which He does, He knows what you need to ready you and your garden for the harvest. So trust Him in every valley and bump in the road along the way. Trust Him even if He has you in dark places at times. God orchestrates every step and season with perfection. He will use every measure to prepare you for the garden of your lifetime. Don't get impatient, and don't settle for less!

How the Poem Was Born

Let the past go. There are blessings beyond what you can ever imagine on the other side of letting go.
—*Author Unknown*

I could call the year 2021 "the year of letting go" for me. The repercussions of losing a spouse before the new year resulted in saying goodbye to my home, car, art studio, and eventually the line of work I'd been in for three years. In the process of selling the house I lived in for four years with my husband, Mike, I also said goodbye to a lot of belongings—furniture, clothing, and many things that I can see now were cluttering up my life and not serving me well anyway.

My 1st husband Vinnie 2008.

I'm quite familiar with "letting go." I've lost two husbands in thirteen years—one to cancer and one to COVID.

Ironically, there's been a lot of similar experiences that took place after both men died. I sold both homes, bought a more suitable house for myself each time, purchased a more reliable vehicle, and started writing.

When my first husband died, a friend introduced me to blogging, which was still pretty new in 2008. I was tired of telling the story over and over again to individuals who heard of Vinnie's death weeks, even months, after he died. Once I started blogging, I could point people to read the blog to learn about the events of the entire year leading up to his death.

I found two things as I was writing each blog post, though, that surprised me. First, I discovered that

Mike and me. Our last Christmas together 2019.

I loved writing. Fortunately, people liked my journaling; and thankfully, composing my reflective thoughts helped me process all that I had experienced that year—every conversation and episode in detail. I found this latter experience very healing.

I also found it helpful to write about what I was experiencing in my first year widowed. It was a rough year. I lost ten other friends and family that year and also lost my employment. As people asked how I was doing, I was thankful for the blog. It was easier to point people to a blog that explained all I was going through than to tell the story repeatedly.

Mike's unexpected decline in strength made his death quite different than Vinnie's. I had time to prepare my heart in some ways for Vinnie's death, but Mike's death was unexpected.

About two months before Vinnie's death, it was clear he would not beat cancer. Instead of seeing progress, we learned it raced destructively through his body and organs very aggressively. While Mike had COPD and was at high risk at age sixty-eight, it seemed he was holding steadily, though weak, during his two-week stay in the hospital. Like the trend of many other COVID-19 patients, the nurses believed that he would suddenly take an upward swing to regain strength in another week or two.

I was hoping he would be home for Christmas, but two days after Christmas, I received a call asking me to decide between keeping him alive or letting him die. How could I answer such a question when I had no idea he would quickly and suddenly decline in strength during the night? I hadn't seen Mike in two weeks. I was not allowed to visit him because he couldn't have visitors due to COVID, and I also had COVID, so I wasn't allowed in the hospital anyway.

I asked the doctor to keep Mike alive until I could get there. Hospital security made special arrangements for me to see him despite us both having COVID. My daughter, also sick with COVID, drove me there. I was in shock and didn't trust myself behind the wheel of a car. I was escorted to the ICU by two police officers, suited up in plastic from head to toe, only to realize that Mike was already gone. Technically he was "alive," but I knew only the medication injected in an artery in his leg was keeping the blood flowing. Minutes later, his blood pressure dropped to 11/13, but I sensed he had already gone home to Jesus before I arrived at the hospital that morning.

The lack of oxygen over the two weeks he was hospitalized eventually started shutting his organs down. In addition, the lack of lung function prevented the body from expelling carbon monoxide. As a result, he died from carbon monoxide poisoning, lack of oxygen, kidney failure, and two heart attacks that morning.

It is no surprise that Mike waited two days after Christmas to die. I imagine him discussing this with God, insisting that he not die on Christmas, just before Christmas or the day after. I suspect Mike would believe that two days after Christmas might lessen the heartache when I think back on Christmas 2020. It didn't, however, reduce the shock, quite honestly. I was widowed again, and I had no idea what was next—except making funeral arrangements.

There was a lot of chaos over the next several weeks. My mother, who had been living with Mike and me for three years, was admitted to the hospital the same afternoon Mike was. She was eighty-six at the time. We were all sick with the virus. Mom, however, came home two days before Christmas. But a week after the holiday, Mom was back in the hospital. This time she had blood clots in her legs and lungs. Those were symptoms of COVID I had not heard of until then. I was having a hard time trying to figure out how I was going to handle everything. It was like standing in the middle of the production of a bad movie. The movie production seemed to be swirling wildly around me; I could hardly focus on one thing and didn't like any of it.

Mom, granddaughter, and me. (2022)
A birthday celebration.

When it was safe for me to come out of quarantine, my sister asked what she could do to help. It wasn't hard to think—I knew what I wanted. I wanted to run away! I didn't tell her that, though, probably because I didn't literally want to run away. I just wanted to get off the wild train ride I was on for a time so I could breathe, think, and rest.

My sister came for a few days to stay with Mom when she was released from the hospital the second time. I stayed in an Airbnb in the next town over—I didn't run very far away! Once again, I found myself writing. It helped me process everything that happened in December—the craziest, saddest December of my life.

I had been in the GriefShare ministry for many years after Vinnie's death. While serving in that ministry, I met other individuals that lost loved ones on, just before, or right after Christmas. Some lost children, and some lost a spouse or a loved one to suicide. Remembering others' grief made mine feel less difficult. I have many things to be thankful for despite the loss of my sweet Michael. I learned so much from my GriefShare experience in the past that helped. Despite my sadness, I couldn't complain; I knew I wasn't alone in my grief.

As I reflected on our ten years together, I found myself thanking God for our marriage. I thought of some very significant reasons God brought us together. Our relationship blessed his last ten years of life while his encouragement, love, and kindness has helped me become all that I need to be in this next chapter of my life. He used to say, "She speeds me up, and I slow her down. God knew we needed that."

When I returned home, I still had an enormous pile of repercussions of his death to deal with, but one thing was sure—God still had me on the planet for a purpose, and Mike wouldn't want anything less for me to pursue. I'll spare you all the details of this year. I'm saving some of those details for another book! But somehow, even in all the craziness, I knew what I needed to do—write more and create more art.

It wasn't the first time I felt a deep urge inside to dive headfirst and with both feet into the world of creating. Two years before Mike died, I attended a conference in Arizona with the company I used to help my independent health coach business. One day at the conference, I heard someone say that health coaching was their whole life. I stopped in my tracks at that moment and realized my identity and destiny in life was not a health coach. While I like helping people, I know that health coaching is not my destiny.

I knew that day in Arizona that I wanted to write and create art. I wanted to be creative my whole life, but no one ever supported me in this dream, so I never pursued it. Of course, I now see that I didn't have the confidence I needed to move forward, but I do now!

Convincing Mike of my new plan after spending money on flights and this conference halfway across the country was challenging. While he believed in the skills God gave me and knew God wanted to use me in these areas, he, like many others (myself included, if I'm honest), didn't believe people could earn a living writing and playing with paint. After all, everyone is familiar with the phrase "starving artist" for a reason. I thought success was for the few super talented for most of my life, but somehow, I started believing it would be part of my new next chapter.

Ironically, after every Sunday morning sermon I attended after that conference, I would tell Mike that it was time for me to walk away from health coaching to start a career in writing and painting. He always said I should find a way to do both—work as a health coach and write or paint on the side. But after Mike died, my new financial situation made me think that there was no better time to try!

"Reflections" 2022. Acrylics. "African Beauty" (2014)
mixed mediums

"Under His Protection" (2022) pastels

I had no idea how to launch a new business in books and art. I'd sold art over the years, and I'd sold about three thousand copies of my first book, but that hardly made me a best seller. I knew I needed help, a coach, or a mentor, or something that could point me in the direction I felt so compelled to go. So of course, I prayed. And lo and behold, God began to answer!

Since that January, I've been introduced to an amazing selection of talented people. I didn't specifically ask for any one of them. I didn't know what to ask for, but God knew! I found a business coach, a Christian artist mentoring community, and a professional artist helping me develop and refine my art. I am also following a successful author's path. She, too, is someone I knew nothing about before 2021. I knew only one of these individuals before this year, and I didn't ask her for help. Instead, she asked me if I'd like her to critique my work and offer tips before she ever knew I prayed for this.

By March, I had a plan to move forward. I would sell the house and move to a townhome to shorten the list of responsibilities once shared with Mike. I had a realtor, family, and mentors to help me make good decisions about my new home and new business pursuit. It felt wonderful to finally have some sense of direction for my future.

One evening I sat down with paper and pen. I didn't have a plan; I just started writing. I was thinking about the harvest I hoped to generate in my new ventures. I thought about the seeds I needed to plant to keep me focused and create the garden I pictured in my mind. But then, what came to me was this poem, *Mary, Dear Mary*—though it didn't have a title until months later.

I wrote and wrote nonstop. Line after line, I was pleased with the flow of words poured out on my paper. But I didn't fall in love with it until I stopped and read it back. Then I wept. Without realizing it until that moment, I had described my journey perfectly. I was about to grow a new garden.

This venture was not going to be the first time I attempted to start a new business. But this time, I had some experience under my belt. I also had a new mindset. I only hoped I would succeed in the past, but deep down, I didn't think I was allowed or capable of success. The old lies of my childhood still haunted me into wondering if I'd ever been good enough to succeed at anything. In the past, I knew God would allow this for others, but I wasn't sure until 2021 that He would use everything I'd ever done to help me build the life of my dreams. Somehow confidence grew, and I could picture my future life.

So *Mary, Dear Mary* was born, all in one swift sitting! I believe God intended it to flow onto paper so easily to build my confidence in His directing my life without Mike. I think the plan is also to encourage other brothers and sisters in Christ to pursue God's plan, for surely we each have a part to play in the Body of Christ. I feel a sense of urgency in these troubling days. There is certainly so much we, as the church, have yet to do, and God can help us do what might seem to be impossible to us!

If you're anything like me, you might overthink what a faith walk might look like for you. I'm sure fear creeps in—and that's okay. Without fear, it wouldn't be a risk and wouldn't take faith and trust in God!

May I encourage you to take time to talk with God after you read the poem? If you feel compelled, ask God what His will is for your life. Start today by rejoicing, thanking Him in all your circumstances, and keep praying. The First Epistle to the Thessalonians 5:16–18 (below) reveals to us that joy, gratitude, and prayer are the bottom line when it comes to fulfilling God's will. So if you're not sure of anything else, at least keep doing these, and the rest will follow.

> Rejoice always, pray continually, and give thanks in all circumstances, for this is God's will for you in Christ Jesus. (1 Thessalonians 5:16–18)

I love these three verses. I fall back on these whenever I'm confused about what to do next. It simplifies life and gets my thinking back on track! But I've also found that when I thank God for the things in my life, I can see threads weaved between the events of my life—even the bad, dark, and hard times. These threads are the lessons and skills learned that God uses to reveal the tapestry He wants to weave, the story He's been wanting us to tell about Him in our life. I can see times where I've cut the threads, but God has an amazing way of tying threads back together seamlessly!

Let me encourage you to spend time praying about your own life and future. Do you often feel like God has something more you're supposed to do in this life? Give it to God. Before you sense His answer, timing, or direction, it might take time, but be persistent in your prayers about it. God will use that willingness, so keep listening and watching what begins taking place in your life as you pray. Then God will start orchestrating what you need, even if it takes years to understand or to see it.

After spending time with God in prayer, do these things:

- Go back and read the poem again.
- Take your time.
- Imagine each stage of the seeds and picture what those seeds might be for you.
- Ask God to show you the harvest and to point you in the direction where you'll find the seeds to sow. Most of them come first from the heart and start with the spirit of thanksgiving and faith. He will show you the rest.

In addition, the last section of this book provides the opportunity to reflect, think carefully, and begin considering what kinds of seeds you want to plant in the days to come. I imagine all of last year's New Year resolutions not executed yet again, nor will they likely be in the coming year. It is silly, isn't it, that we make resolutions without a real plan. So I want to help you think about the different seeds needed to reap a new garden!

It took two years from when I first felt hit in the head with a brick at that conference back in Arizona to when I started writing again and pursuing this new path. During those two years, God was perfectly orchestrating various people and scenarios I had no idea existed! Therefore, let this encourage you to be patient. Keep your God-glasses on so you can detect His fingerprints as he leaves traces for you to see where He is working. Pray often and fear not. Remove doubt because I assure you, God wants to use every person willing to be used for His kingdom! You never have to doubt that!

I can hardly wait to hear your story and hear how I might play some small part in helping launch the passion in your heart to become a full-blazing, unstoppable forest fire!

Mary, Dear Mary
(What's Growing in Your Garden?)

Mary, dear Mary,
    don't be so contrary.
See how your garden could grow!
There's more to life
    than what your eyes can see
    or what you think you know.
Watch each stage of your sowing in seasons
    for God will reveal to you
    how your life is like a garden growing,
    how to live, and what to do.

Seeds planted in deep and dark places
    take time before you see them bloom.
But they'll split wide open
    and appear destroyed
    while the earth shifts to make them room.
    They'll become something bigger
    than what your eyes once saw
    and with care, hard work, and toil,
    soon you'll see and smell the beautiful
    emerge from gritty soil.

Their eager response to the warm, bright sun
will determine how fast they will grow.
And though weeds may emerge to choke them
sometimes making their progress slow,
they'll have a fighting chance to become
the beauty they're meant to be
when destroyers are plucked
and nourishment replenished,
so to flourish and truly grow free.

Before you know it,
    and to your delight,
      your seeds planted with care and love
      become tiny leaves before your eyes
      like hands praising God above.

Watch your seeds and their struggle,
Mary, burst forth
      for they give lessons for you to know how
      to let God use life's troubles and trials
      to live well and in peace here and now.

You may complain of rain at times
        when the weather gets you wet.
But to your little seeds
        inside the ground,
        a basic need is met.
The rain soaks through their hardened shells
        'til they're soft and pliable,
        making room for roots and shoots to grow
        which rain makes reliable.

You'll have weeds in your garden, Mary,
	choking life of what once you thought
	good,
and you'll feel that your life must be over
	because you simply misunderstood
	that the Son is still present above you
	even when your eyes cannot see,
	but the tears you shed in depression
	keep your heart soft so the Lord can be

working His plan for you, Mary,
to be like the garden you desire;
	but first,
trust the struggles, stages, and challenges
before the best of who you are will burst
forth in God's garden, Mary,
revealing who you're meant to be
in this world that needs you, dear Mary,
to bring hope and help set others free.

For many are lonely and in darkness
and it seems they're but forgotten.
They need hope to see the Son shine bright
so they are nourished and not left rotten.

As the rain falls upon them
        and they think that they might drown
        you can bring hope to their lives, Mary,
        where joy can replace their frown.
        As they learn to stay focused on our
        Maker,
        as you have in your own time of despair.
You'll take someone's hand to meet Jesus
        and He will meet you both there.

Rise and shine, oh darling Mary,
    don't be dismayed
        if your garden grows slow.
You'll bloom once more
        though the storm may not clear
        and hard winds begin to blow,

For with God, you'll be strong and
victorious
in His beauty and majesty.
You'll bloom and shine
one day, Mary
for all the world to see.

It always amazes me how much time it takes to get all the tools and materials together for a repair or building project. The same is true of gardening.

One year, Mike and I planted vegetables in large crates raised high enough off the ground that weeding and harvesting would not require bending over. Before we started growing, we had to plan what seeds, soil, tools, natural pesticides, and fertilizer to use, but we also had to paint the crates with outdoor paint, lay blocks for the containers to sit on, and level them all before adding dirt. The project took weeks before we could plant our little seeds!

It takes a lot of thought, time, preparation, and planning to build anything worthwhile—including a garden that will produce a bountiful harvest of any kind. So before we explore and discern your dreams, passions, and purpose on earth (the seeds), we must be sure your mind and heart are ready for the task (the soil).

When my husband and I purchased a truckload of soil for our raised-crate vegetable garden, we spent days sifting, mixing, and preparing it for the seeds. Likewise, the heart and mind need to be healthy, so we are confident in the success of our pursuit.

Do you have the confidence to believe the garden you desire to grow is possible for you? Checking your confidence level is crucial to success. It's the main reason for my success in the business I'm phasing out of and the success I expect in this new venture I'm pursuing.

The purpose of writing this book is to encourage you to pursue your dream role in life. For God's children, that is often a desire that burns in our hearts partly because it is who God made us. As I have grown to understand this in my later years of life, I want to help others see it too—and own it! Unfortunately, it seems far too many people do not believe they have what it takes to succeed in their dream or passion.

Perhaps you have been told (and believed) you aren't worthy or smart enough to succeed at anything. Unfortunately, that was the case for me for decades and is the case for many people, especially women I've known over the years. Even though my season of motherhood was so fulfilling, I still had a nagging feeling that there was something more, something else I was supposed to do on this planet.

One of my female Biblical heroes and role models in the Bible is the Proverbs 31 woman. This last chapter of Proverbs describes a noble wife who fed and clothed her family, servants, and the poor. She was a wonderful mother, wife, and manager—they called her blessed. In addition to the household roles of this tireless woman, she invested in real estate, managed a vineyard, and ran a retail business.

Proverbs 31, though, can give the impression that this powerhouse superhero worked twenty hours a day, cooking, cleaning, and helping their kids do homework while running several businesses. But I'll admit, I've tried to "do it all" and found it challenging to do any one thing well! Therefore, I think it is safe to say she didn't do them all at once. We don't have a time frame for the Proverbs 31 woman, but I think it's safe to say that she didn't do them all in the same year either! Still, this confident lady encourages us to sense all that God has made us capable of pursuing, to fulfill the passions and roles, and use the gifts God gave each of us.

There are several admirable women in the New Testament too. Tabitha, or Dorcas in Greek, continuously abounded with deeds of kindness and charity, especially to the widows. Lydia was a retailer who sold purple cloth. She also led her household to the Lord and hosted the apostles, offering her home a place for them to stay.

Many more admirable women in the Bible inspire us, but let's not forget Mary who sat at Jesus's feet while her cousin scurried around, getting the house ready for guests. Jesus reminds us in this story that we need to listen, learn, and spend time growing our love relationship with Him. Sitting at the feet of Jesus, ladies, is where we find the seeds to grow the passions He wants to help us grow and harvest! It is also how to prepare the heart and mind (the soil).

Looking back at my life, I can see that though I didn't recognize it for many years, I was born with a natural entrepreneurial spirit. I started many little businesses over the years, and though I have never had a big successful corporation, I always had the tenacity to work hard and make money using my skills and abilities.

When I was young, I spent many hours selling lemonade in the neighborhood. I wrote plays and charged family members money for tickets to see the show. At age eleven, I started babysitting, and for years, my sister and I made crafts each summer and sold them to all the people at my mother's office.

I created small wooden key chains and sold them at a flea market when I was a young mom. Then, when my daughters were old enough to start school, I created an assistant admin business to help small businesses that needed help with odds and ends but weren't in a position to hire someone permanently. Later I started a few MLM businesses, started a neighborhood brick and mortar craft shop, and I ran an eBay business on the side.

But the last business I built was a health coach business. While an independent health coach, the company I worked with provided excellent, practical training sessions and encouraged team building. The result was amazing and unlike any other business experience I'd ever had! I established a comfortable income and a team of coaches under me that I truly love. The experience is what I needed to learn how to run my own business doing what I love doing.

Before my health coach business, none of the little business ventures I'd ever started got very far. Some were successful but only for a season. Others fell flat pretty quickly. But I've come to realize one underlying reason for the lack of success or lack of ongoing success: confidence and vision.

I haven't quite put my finger on all the reasons why confidence and vision are crucial to success. But my experience in health coaching made clear to me that these two elements were missing in the past. So before we begin thinking and planning on what new garden you have always wanted to harvest, let's look at these two vital seeds that must come first: confidence and vision.

How Confident Are You?

The first Scripture I referenced at the beginning of this book is Ephesians chapter 4. But it is not the only passage that describes God's gifts to each of His children. For example, chapter twelve in the first book of Corinthians talks specifically about the many spiritual gifts He disperses among His people and how they fit together perfectly as the body of Jesus Christ on earth.

The book of Romans, chapter 12, verse 4, says, "For just as each of us has one body with many members, and these members do not all have the same function, so in Christ, we, though many, form one body, and each member belongs to all the others."

There are others, but I think these three passages clarify that God gives each of His children gifts, talents, experiences, and skills to be used on earth. If that's His desire and His purpose in calling us together as one body, we can be confident that He wants to use us! While imperfect human beings may not be worthy of such a calling, we must be completely sure of our purpose. We are more than able with Him!

As we reflect on the Scriptures, especially as they relate to the garden we want to harvest, we will want to take inventory of what we've always loved to do, what we believe about ourselves, others, God, and more. I will provide you the opportunity to ponder these things in the last of these pages. But before we go there, let's talk a moment about vision. While confidence is important in moving forward, vision points to the specific direction and decisions it will take to grow your new garden.

Do You Have a Dream for the Future?

I praise you, for I am fearfully and wonderfully made. Wonderful are your works; my soul knows it very well. (Psalm 139:14)

When I ask, "Do you have a dream for the future?" I am not referring to the fantasies we sometimes have about places we want to run away to be at peace and completely off-grid from all responsibility. I'm not asking about what you want to do when you retire someday. After all, God still has a plan for us at every age we are in this planet—even during retirement years!

So, consider this instead: God made you with a unique blend of passions, skills, interests, talents, and spiritual gifts (Ps 139:14). These make up the unique way you add value to the world around you. Do you know what that is? Or do you sense there's more and can't put your finger on it?

If you answered yes to the last question, allow me to encourage you to consider a few other questions carefully:

- How and where do you add value to others' lives?
- What do you do that people appreciate about you—those things that make you feel good about yourself?
- To what places and activities do you gravitate?
- What do you tend to volunteer for when the opportunity presents itself?
- Do you have a hobby or activity that you like to do in your free time? (Note: watching television is passive, not a creative activity.)
- Do you have a special talent that you'd love to teach to others?
- Would you like to spend more time doing any or all of these?

I'm quite familiar with each of these questions. I've asked myself and God these questions many times over the years. Yet, ironically, many of the things I have discovered as I've explored the answers to these questions are unveiled talents and skills I didn't know I had.

I mentioned earlier that I spent many hours of my youth crafting, babysitting, making lemonade, and writing plays. Each of these earned me a little money. This trend that came naturally to me as a child has helped me see who and what I am more clearly in the past ten years or so. It's taken forty years to see that the passion and joy in a few simple activities would pave the way to how I'm making a living now! They were so natural for me that I never concluded that they might be unique to the life I am to live today!

You see, whether we realize it or not, we have been programmed at a young age to function in a particular way. Sometimes these are imposed by our culture and sometimes by individuals in our lives. These behavior trends are not always a bad thing. But unfortunately, most people develop them, along with beliefs and triggers as children that unknowingly don't serve them well later in life.

One of the reasons I mentioned Mary earlier, who sat at the feet of Jesus while Martha frantically ran around the house cleaning, is to help see how and why we need to dig deep to see those layers that need to peel away. The way to do it is to sit at the feet of Jesus, to listen, stop, get off our daily merry-go-round, rest, be quiet, learn, and be willing to change. I call this experience "white space."

White space is the opportunity to sift the wheat from the shaft, so to speak—the unique person you truly are from the person you've become that can just as easily change. White space clears the noise and clutter, and it helps remove the whys and hows that don't serve you well anymore to discover who you've always felt deep down in your soul who you are meant to be. This fabulous person you truly are is blended well with unique passions, gifts, and interests that make you feel good about yourself as they also add joy and value to others.

It took many years to understand that many character traits I thought were just part of my unchangeable identity was instilled in me as I was growing up. For instance, when I was younger, I'd start laughing uncontrollably. For years, I thought I was just silly, but I learned later in life that it was a nervous trigger. Eventually, I realized that when I was uncomfortable or stressed, I'd start laughing to the point of tears because I was not allowed to cry when I stressed as a child. Laughter was a good way to express all the stress I bottled up most of the time. That worked when I was young (except at school), but it didn't serve me well as an adult. Therefore, I grew up believing something about myself that wasn't true. Over time, I was able to change the behavior I once thought was unchangeable.

Many character traits are the product of our environments. They are usually defense triggers, behavior, or decisions that we make based on fear. Let me give you another good example.

I know of a woman whose mother never let her play. When her mother saw her playing or being idle, she would tell her that she needed to do more chores if she had nothing to do. As a result, she couldn't sit down for more than ten minutes as an adult without feeling like she had to jump out of her chair and clean something.

She lived her whole life that way—never having the opportunity to explore any other ways she might add joy to others in her life. Certainly, there were people in her life that would have enjoyed just spending more time with her! Some may have commended her for not being lazy; that's a good trait. But the belief system drilled into her mind as a child didn't serve her well later in life—it crippled her relationships with others and robbed her of activities that would have brought her greater joy and blessed many others.

While my stepfather was very strict and overpowering, and I had many chores and responsibilities as a child (which I don't regret!), I was also home alone for long periods. Time alone at home gave me the time I might not have otherwise had to play, and now I can see how vitally important the balance of play and chores was in my childhood. I am grateful for that and for my other friends and relatives who saw potential in me; their encouragement blessed me in ways I didn't see for many years.

Perhaps you haven't had individuals in your life that allowed you space to discover unique gifts, passions, and talents built into your DNA. If that's the case, I want you to know that it is not too late for you! I'm sixty-five years old; it's only been a few years since I began to recognize and put together all the common threads that have been weaving my overall story! If this happened to me, it most certainly could happen to you too!

Let's go back to the questions I asked earlier. This time I suggest you think about each one carefully and start writing down your thoughts in a notepad, journal, or notebook. I have not provided space for you to write in this book because I don't want to limit the area you need to gain the most from the exercise. If it takes ten pages to reveal passions and interests that have been hiding in your heart for decades, I don't want to restrain you by only providing a few lines!

Please, friend, don't rush through the questions. It may be best to consider each question for a few days before moving on to the next. But, of course, you may go back to each question again and again for years—and that's okay! I did that with similar questions after my first husband died, and the results grew into my first book!

I'm not expecting or suggesting you write a book, but I encourage you to work at a pace that feels right for you and be thorough without limiting all you need to see that's been inside you. There's no rule here, just suggestions. Persistently pursuing the process needs to become an ongoing conversation you have between you and God.

He knows everything inside you that is His, and all that is weed! And, speaking of weeds, let me remind you how weeds work in the garden.

When I was a little girl, I remember helping my aunt weed her flower garden. She had lovely flowers, and I was happy to help—to an extent. I wouldn't say I liked seeing the ugly weeds, but I didn't particularly appreciate getting my hands dirty either. Trying to grab all of the roots took determination and persistent digging that I didn't have! Also, I hated the dirt under my fingernails—even under short nails bitten down to the quick!

Often I would pull off the tops of the weeds, right to the ground, which gave the appearance of no weeds left behind. But a few days later, it was clear that I never got those roots! (This might sound like the way we make those New Year resolutions!)

Allowing God to dig deep into our heart, mind, and soul isn't always pleasant. Getting to the root of things in our past often brings back the emotion of the original incident. The work it takes to relearn and reprocess our history is especially difficult if you didn't learn how to process hurts or trauma experienced as a child. However, if no one equipped you through life's struggles, grief, and the experiences that seemed unfair as a child by giving you permission to grieve and process, there is still good news for you. Our Heavenly Father can teach us at any age, and He is so gracious too!

Remember the seven questions I asked earlier? We are going to revisit these with a bit more insight. The way you approach your answers to these questions may reveal some of your unique makeup, so don't try to make it fit in someone else's box! And I hope you are eager to start digging deep into your heart and mind. But before you do, I have just a few more suggestions that may help:

1. I suggest you take your time to think and respond to each question thoroughly. Please don't feel like you have to write a book. You don't have to write sentences either. If you do not like to write, you won't get far if you write full sentences. You will do well to write down a word or two, or a phrase, that represents a full thought. As long as you know what the word describes, that's enough. The idea here is to get the clutter out of the brain and on to white paper so your pad or notebook gets filled up, and the brain embraces the white space to discern a few things from God!

2. Please pray over these questions and the answers you jot down. God knows more about you than you do. He made you! Ask Him to give you ears to hear, wisdom to discern, and eyes to see threads weaved into the tapestry He calls You. God already knows the answers so, stop, close your eyes, imagine your brain as a file cabinet. Ask God to find the files; then ask how to put them all in order. Take note of what comes

to mind even if it doesn't make sense in the beginning. Not everything will be from God, but it all has to be seen, sorted, and even eliminated to create a better working system of discernment.

3. Ask friends to help you answer some of these questions. Their insight will be very helpful. I am still close to one of my best friends from middle school. While I think I've changed dramatically over the years, she does not. She claims she's always seen the person I am today. I believe God gave her His glasses to wear when we were together in our youth because she remembers someone I didn't meet until late in life!

Let me share another example of what can happen when you ask friends and family to help you in the process of defining the true you and your potential purpose on earth.

Part of joining my first church back in 1994 was to take a spiritual gift test. I will admit that I was disappointed at first to see that my strongest spiritual gift is faith. I wanted it to be administration or teaching. Those would make it easy to know where and how to serve the church. But I had no idea how the gift of faith played a part in building up the body of Christ—that is, until I talked with a very wise lady, Dolores.

Dolores was the leader of the first Bible study I ever attended. She asked me one day what the spiritual gift test revealed. My face probably had my disappointment written all over it, but I proceeded to tell her I ranked strongest in faith.

Though my face expressed my frustrated feelings, hers suddenly had an expression of delight! When I asked why the excitement and how faith fits in the church, she explained: People with strong faith need to be at every prayer meeting to encourage those lacking faith. They need to remind others that God can do what seems impossible to us.

Her excitement and explanation helped me to never feel disappointed again about my spiritual gift. Talking with a friend helped me tremendously that day to see how I am to serve the church and live life. I still need to seek the ministries that most need my sprinkle of faith in each new season of my journey, but knowing why it is essential creates a tremendous starting point.

Some of your friends and family may also be wearing those God-glasses and see who you truly are, so don't be afraid to ask them for their insight. Okay, let's return to our fourth suggestion.

4. Over the years, many seeds have produced a good, desirable harvest while others have grown weeds. Yet there are still seeds to sow that will allow you to thrive in your garden and produce abundance that blesses your soul and the lives of many others. Therefore I urge you to go back and read the poem, again and again, each time prayerfully ask-

ing the Lord to reveal to you what you need to do to see the garden you both desire. I believe the poem will help you in the process of reaching deep in your heart and God's for answers.

The seven questions we will review again on the following page will reveal many things if you keep working on them. However, after working through your answers, you may want to dig deeper. In that case, you may explore the additional suggestions I added at the end of the book. But it will make more sense to work through those after doing some soul searching through these initial questions.

Seven Questions to Help Prepare Your New Garden

Are you ready? Let's thoughtfully, honestly, and carefully reflect on the answers to these questions I asked earlier. There are many others to be asked, and you may think of and answer some of your own. My hope, however, is that these will get you started. Let's begin.

1. How and where do you add value to others' lives?
2. What do you do that people appreciate about you, those things that make you feel good about yourself?

3. To what places and types of activities do you gravitate?
4. What do you tend to volunteer for when the opportunity presents itself?
5. Do you have a hobby or activity you like to do in your free time? (Note: watching television is passive, not a creative activity.)
6. Do you have a special talent that you'd love to teach to others?
7. Would you like to spend more time doing any or all of these?

Additional Exercises

When you believe you thoroughly answered the questions in the previous section (though you will want to revisit them periodically), you may find that you have a clearer plan for your future, or you might still be feeling clueless. If you are like me in any way, you may have a nagging feeling that there is more you are meant to be or do in your life but can't quite get your finger on it.

I felt like God dropped hints for me in many different seasons of my life's journey, but until I took a long serious look, I didn't see how to connect those hints or create steps to see the full picture. I was surprised to eventually find talents I didn't realize I had all along because they were so second nature to me—I paid little attention to them.

So I'd like to share some scriptures (at the end of the book) that might help you think about who

God says you are in Christ Jesus. You will need to pray for God's heart if you don't believe any or some of the descriptions. God loves to show you His heart so pray earnestly. He will help you see yourself as He does. And, my fabulous friend, if you need permission to think fondly of yourself, I give it to you right now! Knowing God's heart for you is crucial to understanding what will ultimately bless your life and others. You really can't understand how to love others until you've accepted the purest, deepest love there is—God's gift of love for you!

I also want to encourage you to explore your interests—old or new. I've had individuals tell me they aren't creative, yet after attending an art workshop a few times, they began creating art for themselves and their friends! Of course, that's one example, but you may never know what you can do until you do it a few times! So grab a friend, dig up a spirit of adventure, and try new things. It is more beneficial to say no to something you've attempted than to say no to things you're only assuming you can't do well.

Another great tool is a vision board. You will solidify what you "see" in your future by creating a vision board. It doesn't require art skills—you can cut, paste, or tape pictures from computer printouts, photos, and magazines. Visualizing what you'd like to do will help you think of ways and times to set goals and begin planning.

In the same way that writing words on a blank page helps clear white space in the brain, seeing images on paper will have equal benefit. Think like an architect. He draws out the plan before he gathers the materials and the workforce to build. All that must take place before the building begins. Visualizing the garden you desire will help you too!

When you have time, shop for a large poster board. I suggest a thick board that will hold up in humidity and much activity. Then stay busy arranging and rearranging this board throughout the year, especially as you discover new things by exploring new activities or allowing the Scriptures to renew your heart and mind!

Find pictures that represent various things in your vision. For instance, if you desire a peaceful garden free of worry, perhaps you'll find photos (in your photo collection, on *Google*, or in magazines or books) like a sunset, mountains, or soft waves at the beach. The picture doesn't have to make sense to anyone but you. You can write a word or two over it or under it if that helps you remember what it represents.

The idea behind the vision board is to start where you are at now. The board can change over time. I hope it does! Life is not stagnant, and if you're living your fullest life, you won't be dormant at any stage of your life—and your vision board will have continued changes too!

I know I have mentioned a few times to take your time. I can't encourage you enough times to be patient. Did you know some plants don't reach their peak harvest for years? I once watched a documentary about plants on the peaks of Mount Kilimanjaro. One of the flowering plants takes seven years to bloom, and that is by God's design! Let this be a reminder that the most beautiful gardens take continuous work and patience!

There is no rush, my friend. Instead, I hope you will find that the journey is as much joy and fulfillment as the harvest so you learn to enjoy every single stage of your life—even the hard seasons. Each season helps you produce a more amazing and abundant garden that will bless your socks off and the socks of those around you too!

As you work on discovering your passions, skills, talents and gifts, and partner with your Maker to create the life you both desire for you, you may find you need to plant some seeds earlier than others. For example, you might need to return to school or find a coach, a prayer partner, a mentor, an accountability partner—or perhaps all of these. Be sure to include them in your vision board and journal! Start with everything you think of because you can always eliminate some of them later.

The journey makes life as exciting as the harvest. The harvest is simply the celebration of the work done along the way—a celebration many get to partake in with you. Live well. Learn much—especially in the hardest seasons. They all play a part in removing that which has been hiding your brilliant shine. Allow life's hardships to be like sandpaper that not only grinds you down to the diamond you truly are but also cuts out the facets that make you shine brightest!

Who You Are in Christ

As promised, at the end of the book, I added a brief list of some biblical references to help you understand who you are in Christ Jesus. It is not an exhaustive list; it is a simple basic start. After reading through the list, pick out the ones that resonate most with you and look up their references in the Bible. Then I suggest you read the entire chapter. It is helpful to also read a variety of translations to gain even more insight and understanding. I like using *Bible Gateway* because it is easy to compare a variety of translations quickly. You type the scripture reference in the search box, then select each translation from the many listed. This exercise takes time, but the more time you take, the more you will learn about God and His heart.

Read these daily, personalize each one, memorize them, and don't forget to thank God that He made you in all the ways described below and more!

- I bear fruit in my life because I live in Christ and He in me (John 15:5).
- I will never be left alone or forsaken (Hebrews 13:5b).
- His power gives me strength even in my weakness (2 Corinthians 12:10).
- The Spirit lives in me; I am the temple of the living God (2 Corinthians 6:16).

- God who lives in me is greater than this world (1 John 4:4).
- I have the gifts or the fruit of the Spirit: love, joy, peace, patience, kindness, goodness, faithfulness, gentleness, and self-control (Galatians 5:22–23).
- I am made in the image and likeness of God (Genesis 1:27).
- I have the Spirit of God to know the mind and will of God for my life (1 Corinthians 2:12).
- The Lord makes my steps firm for I delight in Him (Psalm 37:23).
- I have spiritual gifts that together with other Believers, make up the body of Christ (1 Corinthians 12:12).
- I am made righteousness because of Christ Jesus (2 Corinthians 5:21).
- Jesus is my Living Water so I will never thirst again (John 7:37).
- I have been chosen by God to bear lasting fruit in this world (John 15:16).
- I am a new creation in Christ Jesus (2 Corinthians 5:17).
- I am redeemed and forgiven of my sins because of the grace of God (Ephesians 1:7).
- I am fearfully and wonderfully made (Psalm 139:14).

- I am chosen to be a special royal priesthood of God to praise Him and live in His light (1 Peter 2:9).

As you continue to explore God's Word, you may want to add to the list I've provided. And though this book is short, I hope I have given you plenty to ponder for quite a while. But, please don't let it overwhelm you! Instead, stay committed to doing a little at a time each day, preferably at the same time each day, to create a habit for the weeks, months, and even the years ahead. Remember that thorough preparation will create a thriving garden. Keep digging out weeds; don't just appear ready by simply pulling off the tops because the roots that remain will continue to choke your garden, and your harvest will wither away quickly.

You have what it takes to do the work without my help, but I hope you now have plenty to work on to prepare for the most amazing season of your life. Be patient. Keep learning; after all, we never want to think we've learned everything there is to know about God! And most of all, persevere for our faith is often tested. However, I assure you, God loves you. He has a purpose for your life that grows you and glorifies Him. The garden will be abundant—keep believing!

Gail Ruth Peterson is an author, artist, teacher, and speaker. Many trials, losses, grief, hardship, and trouble fuel her passion to write and share stories that truly inspire many with hope and renewed faith. Gail Ruth is also an art teacher, providing opportunities for people to explore their creativity, learn to relax, relieve stress, and gain confidence and joy as they understand who God intended them to be more deeply.

Gail lives in central North Carolina with easy access to the ocean and mountains, which are key places of meditation, healing, reflection, time with the Lord, and inspiration for art and writing.